Crafts for
Christmas

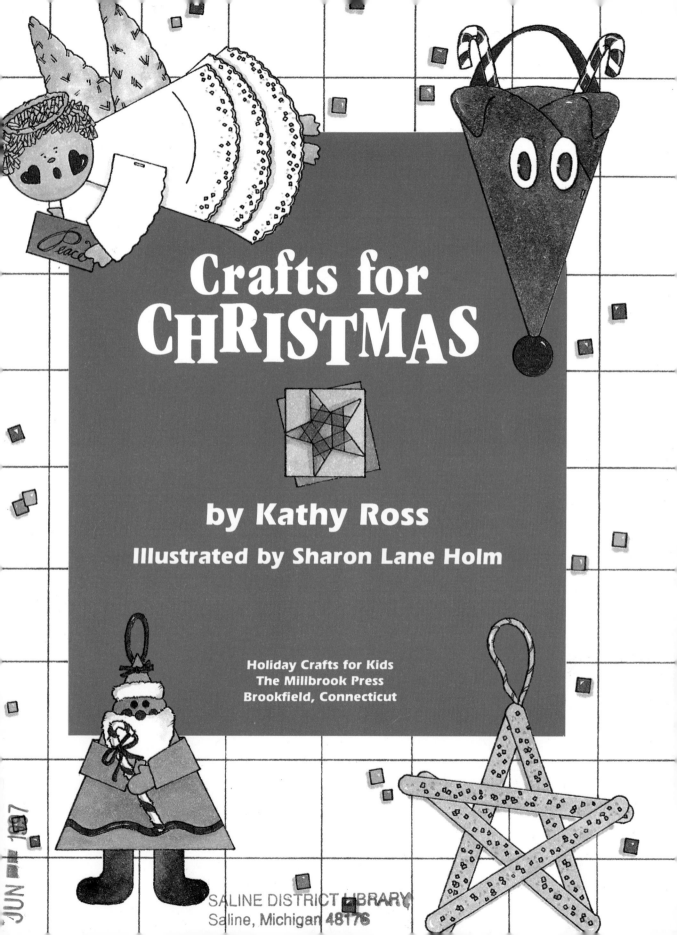

Crafts for CHRISTMAS

by Kathy Ross

Illustrated by Sharon Lane Holm

Holiday Crafts for Kids
The Millbrook Press
Brookfield, Connecticut

To Greyson and Allison—K.R.
To Michael—S.L.H.

Library of Congress Cataloging-in-Publication Data
Ross, Kathy (Katharine Reynolds), 1948–
Crafts for Christmas / by Kathy Ross;
illustrated by Sharon Lane Holm
p. cm. —(Holiday crafts for kids)
Summary: Presents twenty simple crafts that young
children can make from everyday materials.
ISBN 1-56294-536-X (lib. bdg.) ISBN 1-56294-681-1 (pbk.)
1. Christmas decorations—Juvenile literature.
2. Handicraft—Juvenile literature. [1. Christmas
decorations. 2. Handicraft.] I. Holm, Sharon Lane, ill.
II. Title. III. Series.
TT900.C4R677 1995 745.594'12—dc20 94-48304 CIP AC

Published by The Millbrook Press
2 Old New Milford Road
Brookfield, Connecticut 06804

Copyright © 1995 by Kathy Ross

Contents

Merry Christmas!

For Christians throughout the world Christmas is a celebration of great joy and hope because it is the birthday of Jesus, whom Christians believe to be the Son of God. Because the customs of the season are so popular and widely followed, many people celebrate the positive spirit of this holiday even though they may not embrace its specific religious beliefs.

The month of December is full of preparations for the big day on December 25. Families around the world have special Christmas traditions. Wreaths may be hung on front doors, and trees may be decorated both indoors and outdoors. Special Christmas cookies and other foods are often prepared, and presents are purchased or made and wrapped to be placed under the tree.

Small children try to be extra good in hopes of a visit from Santa Claus. They believe that Santa will come in a sleigh pulled by flying reindeer and bring special toys made by the elves at his North Pole workshop.

Whether celebrated as a religious holiday, as a traditional holiday, or as both, Christmas can be a wonderful, exciting, and very busy time for both young and old.

Egg Carton Advent Calendar

An Advent calendar helps you count how many days are left until Christmas.

Here is what you need:

- two cardboard egg cartons
- green poster paint
- red construction paper
- paintbrush
- red yarn
- scissors
- black marker
- white glue
- hole punch
- newspaper to work on

Here is what you do:

1. Cut the lid and closing flap off two matching cardboard egg cartons and save them for another project.

2. Spread out some newspaper to work on, and paint the bottoms of the egg cartons green on both sides. Let them dry.

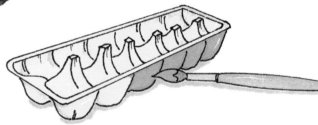

3. Punch two holes on one side of each of the egg cartons and tie them together with a piece of yarn. Do not tie the yarn

so tight that the cartons will not open and close. Punch a hole in the top of each carton and tie the two ends of a piece of yarn through the holes so that the calendar can be hung up. Punch a hole on the outer side of each carton and tie a piece of yarn through each hole so that the calendar can be closed and tied together.

4. Cut twenty-four circles from red construction paper that just fit over the top of each of the openings. Number them from one to twenty-four.

5. Fill each compartment of the egg carton with a tiny surprise. You can use wrapped candy, coins, stickers, tiny toys, or ornaments, and little pieces of paper with promises of a special favor or surprise. Put a dab of glue on two sides of each compartment and cover each with a red circle, starting with number one over the first compartment and ending with number twenty-four. Tie the calendar shut. It is ready to give to someone you know who is counting the days until Christmas.

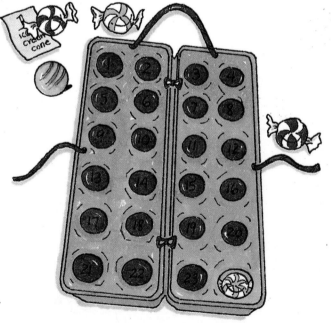

Get together with lots of friends to make and fill these calendars and then trade them for a surprise each day until Christmas.

Stick Star Tree Ornament

A bright star appeared over the stable where the Baby Jesus was born, showing the way to those who came to see Him.

Here is what you need:

five craft sticks

yellow poster paint

paintbrush

gold glitter

white glue

paper cup

newspaper to work on

an empty jar to dry the star on

3-inch (about 7.5-centimeter) piece of yellow yarn

Here is what you do:

1. Arrange the sticks on newspaper to form a star shape just as you would if you were drawing a five-pointed star on paper without lifting your pencil. Put a dab of glue under each of the points that touch on the star and let the glue dry.

2. Pour a small amount of paint into a paper cup and add a tablespoon of white glue. Mix it well. Paint the star yellow on both sides and immediately sprinkle both sides with gold glitter. Carefully balance it on top of a glass jar to dry. Glue a loop of yellow yarn to one of the points so you can hang the star on your Christmas tree.

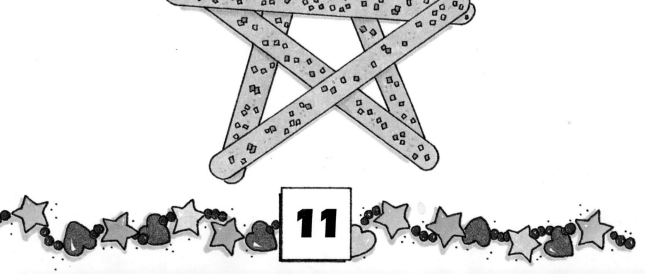

Three Kings Banner

Three wise men came to visit the Baby Jesus, bringing
Him gifts of gold, frankincense, and myrrh.

Here is what you need:

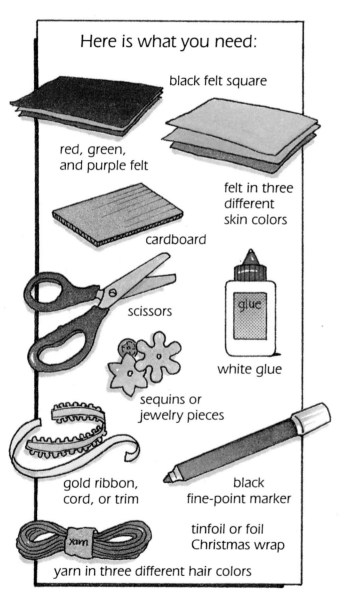

black felt square

red, green,
and purple felt

felt in three
different
skin colors

cardboard

scissors

white glue

sequins or
jewelry pieces

gold ribbon,
cord, or trim

black
fine-point marker

tinfoil or foil
Christmas wrap

yarn in three different hair colors

Here is what you do:

1. Cut tall triangles from red, green, and purple felt to make the bodies of the three kings. Cut a head for each king from felt of a different skin shade. Arrange them on the black felt with the triangles slightly overlapping each other.

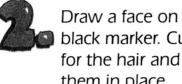 Draw a face on each king with a black marker. Cut up bits of yarn for the hair and beards, and glue them in place.

Cut crowns from foil and glue one on each king. Glue a jewel or cluster of sequins on the front of each king for a gift. You can also decorate their crowns and robes with gold ribbon, cord, trim, and sequins.

Cut a 1-inch (2.5-centimeter) strip of cardboard as long as the top of your banner. Cover both sides of the cardboard with glue and fold the top of the banner back over it to keep the banner stiff when you hang it.

Tuck the end of some gold cord or ribbon under the glue flap at each end of the banner and let the glue dry.

Flying Angel

Angels told of the birth of the Baby Jesus.

Here is what you need:

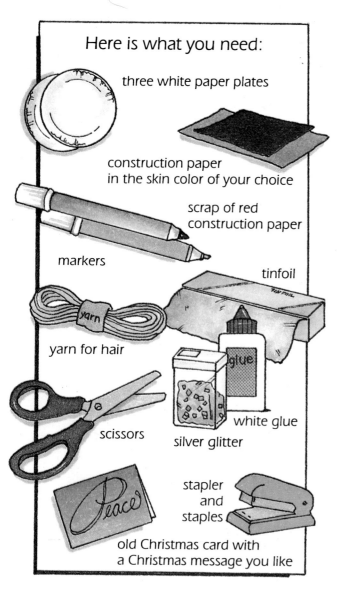

three white paper plates

construction paper
in the skin color of your choice

scrap of red
construction paper

markers

tinfoil

yarn for hair

scissors

silver glitter

white glue

stapler
and
staples

old Christmas card with
a Christmas message you like

Here is what you do:

1. Stack the three paper plates so that the rims are layered to one side and staple them together. Turn the plates over and cut from the layered rims up to a point on each side. This will make the angel dress. Cut two sleeves from the scraps and staple one to each side so that they are hanging down. Cut wings from the scraps and wrap them in tinfoil. Staple them to the top back of the angel.

2. Cut hands, feet, and a head for the angel from construction paper. Draw a face on the angel's head with markers. Cut heart-shaped cheeks from red paper and glue them in place. Cut bits of yarn for hair and glue them on. Squeeze a strip of tinfoil into the shape of a halo and glue it to the top of the angel's head. Glue the hands and feet in place.

3. Decorate the angel's dress with silver glitter. Cut a Christmas message from an old Christmas card and glue it between the angel's hands.

hands   feet

Jar Candleholder

Candles at Christmas represent the light brought into
the world by the birth of the Baby Jesus.

Here is what you need:

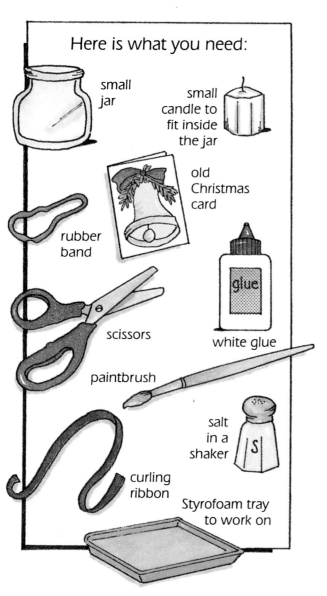

small
jar

small
candle to
fit inside
the jar

old
Christmas
card

rubber
band

scissors

white glue

paintbrush

salt
in a
shaker

curling
ribbon

Styrofoam tray
to work on

Here is what you do:

1. Cut out a pretty picture from an old Christmas card; it should be small enough to fit on the side of the jar. Cover the back of the picture with glue, and glue it on the jar. Put a rubber band around the jar to hold the picture in place until the glue dries.

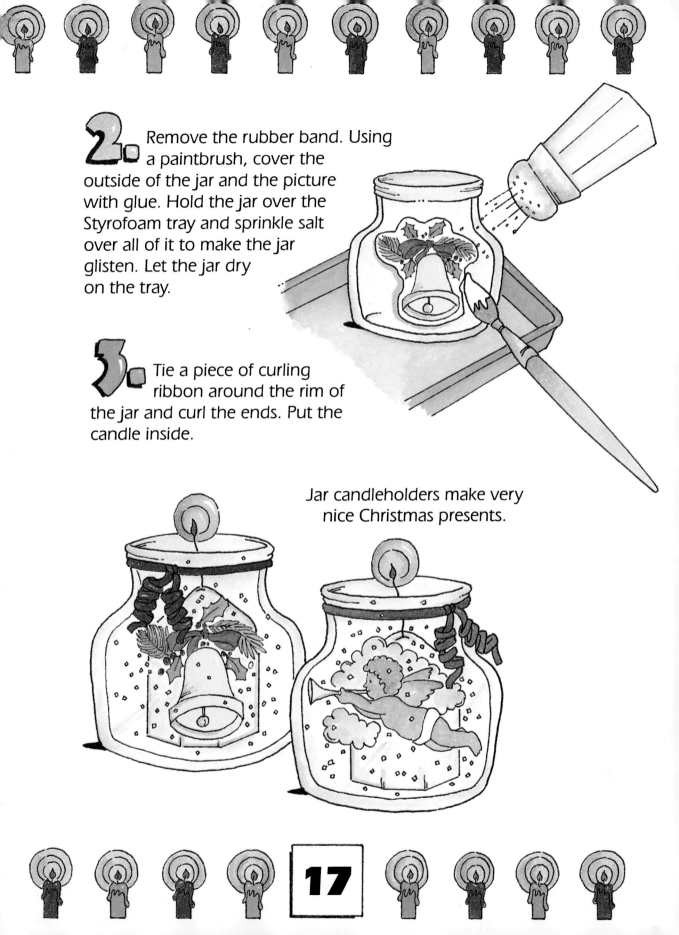

2. Remove the rubber band. Using a paintbrush, cover the outside of the jar and the picture with glue. Hold the jar over the Styrofoam tray and sprinkle salt over all of it to make the jar glisten. Let the jar dry on the tray.

3. Tie a piece of curling ribbon around the rim of the jar and curl the ends. Put the candle inside.

Jar candleholders make very nice Christmas presents.

Christmas Story Pieces

The story of the birth of Baby Jesus is loved by all Christians, young and old, and is at the very center of the Christmas celebration. You can enact the story over and over again with this project.

Here is what you need:

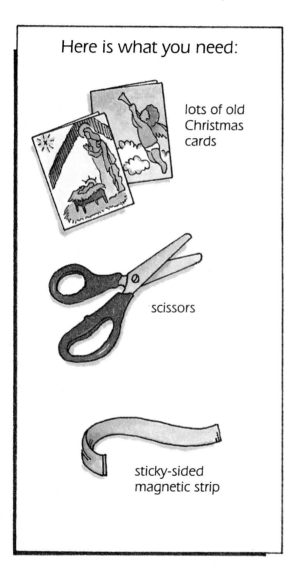

lots of old Christmas cards

scissors

sticky-sided magnetic strip

Here is what you do:

1. Look through old Christmas cards to find nice, large pictures of all the people and animals that were part of the Christmas story. You will need pictures of Mary and Joseph and the Baby Jesus, plus the shepherds, angels, wise men, sheep, camels, and whatever other animals you would like to include.

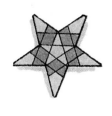   

2. Cut carefully around each picture and stick a small piece of magnet on its back. You can arrange and play with your pictures on a refrigerator door or a cookie sheet.

Egg Carton Christmas Tree

At Christmastime, people often bring pine or fir trees into their homes and decorate them.

Here is what you need:

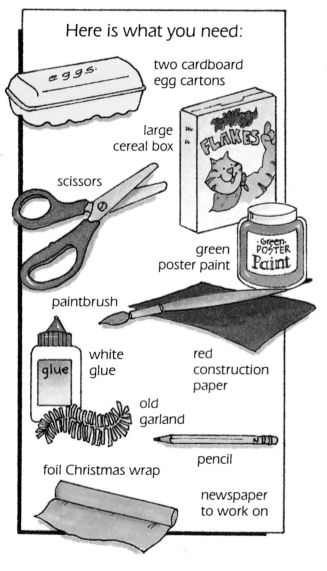

two cardboard egg cartons

large cereal box

scissors

green poster paint

paintbrush

white glue

red construction paper

old garland

foil Christmas wrap

pencil

newspaper to work on

Here is what you do:

1. Open the top and bottom of the cereal box and tear the seams open so that you have a flat piece of cardboard. Cut the egg carton cups into rows of one, two, three, four, five, and six cups. Arrange the cups on the cardboard from the longest row at the bottom to the single cup at the top to form the triangle shape of a tree. Trace around the cups with a pencil and draw a tree trunk at the bottom. Cut the tree shape out of the cardboard.

2. Cover the cardboard with glue and arrange the egg cups again on the cardboard to form a tree. Put something heavy, like a book, on top of the egg cups to help the tree dry flat.

3. Paint the tree green and let it dry.

4. Squeeze glue between all the rows of the tree and press the garland between the rows. Cut a small piece of garland to glue to the trunk of the tree. Use foil wrap and construction paper to make ornaments for each of the cups on your tree. Cut a star for the top and glue the star and ornaments in place.

This tree would look great on your front door.

Glitter and Sugar Ornament

Make lots of pretty ornaments to decorate your Christmas tree.

Here is what you need:

bowl

measuring cup

water

sugar

teaspoon

white glue

glitter in any color but clear

scissors

cookie cutters with backs

blue yarn

Here is what you do:

1. Pour 1/2 cup (about 120 milliliters) of sugar into a bowl. Add 1 teaspoon (about 5 milliliters) of glitter and mix well. Add 1 teaspoon (5 milliliters) of water and mix until the sugar is evenly moist.

2. Press the sugar into the cookie cutter, and then tap the ornament gently onto a plate. You should have enough sugar to make about four ornaments. Let them dry hard overnight.

3. When they are completely dry, glue a loop of yarn to the back of each one for a hanger.

Matchbox Present Ornament

At Christmastime, people exchange presents. Here is a present that goes on the tree instead of under it.

Here is what you need:

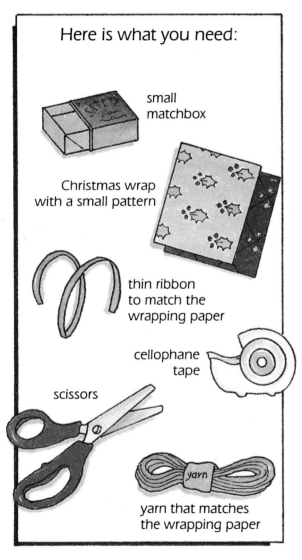

small matchbox

Christmas wrap with a small pattern

thin ribbon to match the wrapping paper

cellophane tape

scissors

yarn that matches the wrapping paper

Here is what you do:

1. Wrap the matchbox just as you would a present. Tie the ribbon around the tiny package and tie a bow.

2. Slip a piece of yarn under the ribbon and tie the two ends together to make a hanger.

Make lots of different package ornaments for your tree.

Ornament Necklace

This ornament hangs on you instead
of on the Christmas tree.

Here is what you need:

pry-off bottle cap

red nail polish

small metal nut

hairpin

red construction paper

scissors

white glue

thin green ribbon

gold rickrack

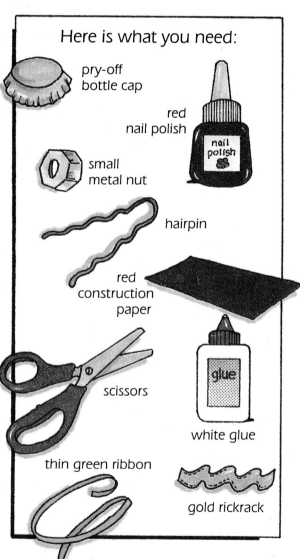

Here is what you do:

1. Paint the outside of the bottle cap with red nail polish and let it dry.

2. Slide the metal nut over the top of the hairpin so that it looks like the hook on the top of a real ornament. Fill the inside of the bottle cap with white glue and bend the ends of the hairpin to fit inside the cap, with the nut and the top of the hairpin sticking out of the edge of the cap.

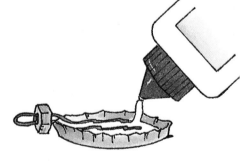

3. Cover the glue in the cap with a circle of red construction paper. Let it dry overnight.

4. Cut a piece of gold rickrack or other trim you might have and glue it across the front of the ornament.

5. Cut a piece of green ribbon the length you would like your necklace to be and thread it through the hairpin. Tie the two ends together to form a necklace.

Grass Wreath

At Christmastime, people often hang wreaths on their front doors to welcome visitors.

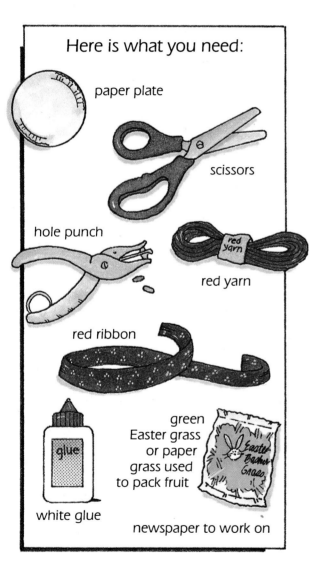

Here is what you need:

paper plate

scissors

hole punch

red yarn

red ribbon

white glue

green Easter grass or paper grass used to pack fruit

newspaper to work on

Here is what you do:

1. Cut the center out of a paper plate. Punch a hole in the rim of the plate and tie a piece of red yarn through for a hanger.

2. Cover both sides of the plate with glue. Cover both sides with the grass. Glue on a pretty Christmas ribbon. Let the wreath dry on a flat surface.

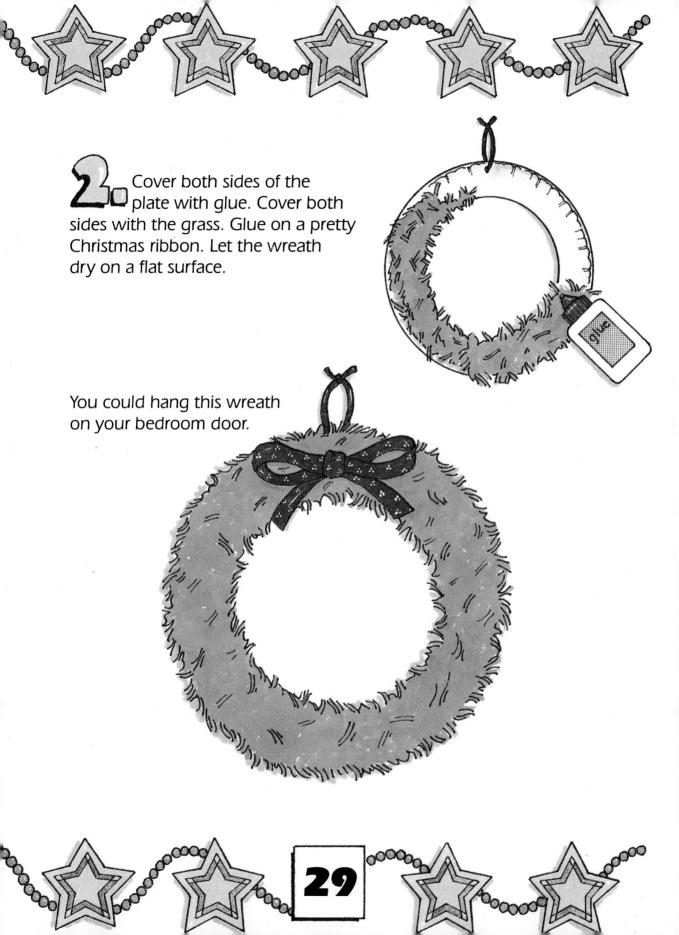

You could hang this wreath on your bedroom door.

Rice Wreath Ornament

This tiny wreath hangs on the Christmas tree.

Here is what you need:

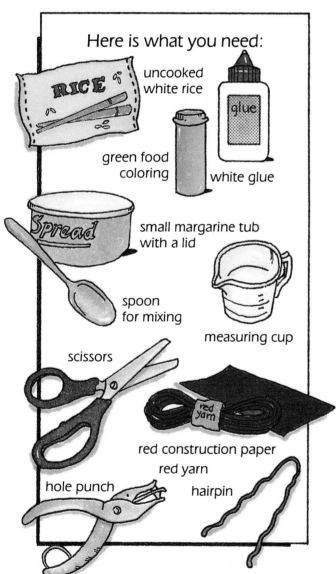

uncooked white rice

green food coloring

white glue

small margarine tub with a lid

spoon for mixing

measuring cup

scissors

red construction paper

red yarn

hole punch

hairpin

Here is what you do:

1. Pour three drops of green food coloring into 1/4 cup (60 milliliters) of glue and mix until the glue is evenly colored. Pour 1/2 cup (about 120 milliliters) of rice into the margarine tub, add the glue, and mix until the rice is completely coated with the green glue.

2. Spoon the rice mixture onto the margarine tub lid and shape it into a wreath. Push a hairpin into the edge of the wreath for a hanger and let the wreath dry overnight.

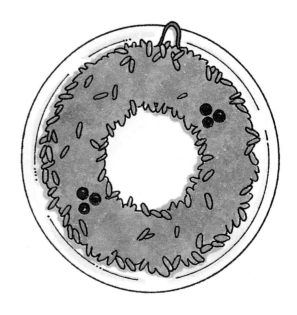

3. With a hole punch, punch berries from red construction paper and glue them on the wreath. Tie a yarn bow and glue it to the top of the wreath.

Santa Door Decoration

Children wait for Santa Claus to bring them presents to open on Christmas morning.

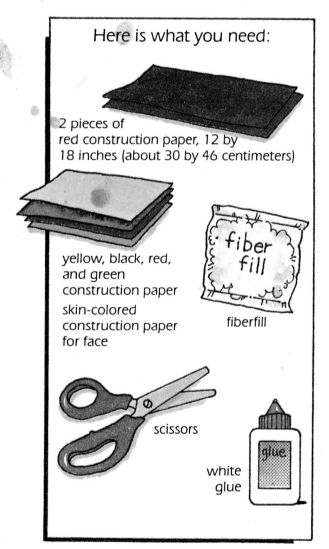

Here is what you need:

2 pieces of red construction paper, 12 by 18 inches (about 30 by 46 centimeters)

yellow, black, red, and green construction paper

skin-colored construction paper for face

fiber fill

fiberfill

scissors

white glue

Here is what you do:

1. Cut the two large sheets of red construction paper in half lengthwise. Glue two of the strips together at the top to form two legs. Glue another strip across the top of the legs to form arms.

2. Cut boots from black paper and mittens from green paper and glue them in place. Cut a face from skin-colored paper and glue it at the top of the body. Cut and glue on a red triangle hat and a black belt with a yellow buckle.

3. Glue fiberfill at the cuffs of the suit and on the rim and at the point of the hat. Glue a big fiberfill beard on the face.

4. Cut eyes from black paper and a nose and cheeks from red paper and glue them on for a face.

This Santa looks great holding a strip of ribbon, tiny lights, or a garland. Just tape an end of the ribbon, lights, or garland to each of the mittens.

Santa Claus Mask

Would you like to be Santa Claus?

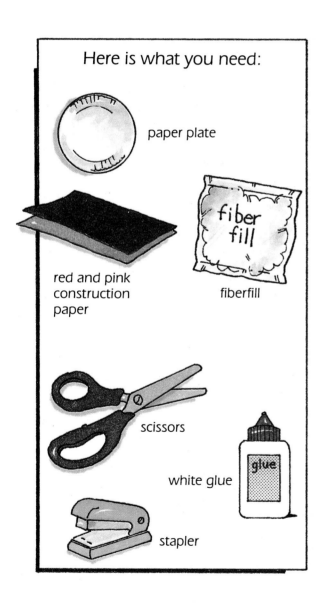

Here is what you need:

paper plate

red and pink construction paper

fiberfill

scissors

white glue

stapler

Here is what you do:

1. Cut the center out of the paper plate and save the rim. Cut out a red triangle hat from the construction paper and glue it to the top of the rim. Glue a fiberfill ball at the point of the hat and a strip of fiberfill along the bottom of the hat.

2. Glue fiberfill all around the rim of the plate to make Santa's beard. Cut out pink cheeks and a red nose and glue them in place.

3. Staple the ends of a strip of red paper to each side of the back of the mask so that the strip forms a band to hold the mask in place.

What would you do if you were Santa Claus?

Stocking Game

Children hang up their stockings on Christmas Eve,
hoping that Santa Claus will fill them with surprises.
This stocking is one you try to fill yourself.

Here is what you need:

long sock

tall cardboard potato chip can

scissors

fiber fill

cotton balls or fiberfill for stuffing

white glue

hole punch

18-inch (46-centimeter) piece of red yarn

small toy

drinking glass that fits only part of the way into the can

Here is what you do:

1. Stuff the foot of the sock, leaving the heel portion empty. Push the can into the sock so that the bottom of the can fills the heel portion of the foot. Pull the sock up over the can as far as it will go and trim the top of the sock so that about 1 1/2 inches (about 4 centimeters) of it extends over the top of the can.

 2. Rub glue around the inside rim of the can and fold the extra sock material over the rim to the inside of the can. Slide the drinking glass into the top of the can to hold the sock in place until the glue dries, then remove the glass.

3. Punch a hole in the top of the can. Tie one end of the yarn through the hole. Tie a small toy to the other end of the yarn.

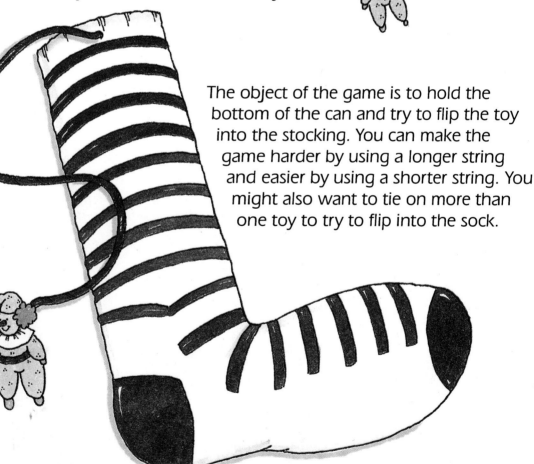

The object of the game is to hold the bottom of the can and try to flip the toy into the stocking. You can make the game harder by using a longer string and easier by using a shorter string. You might also want to tie on more than one toy to try to flip into the sock.

Triangle Elf Ornament

Stories say that elves help Santa Claus make all those toys for good boys and girls.

Here is what you need:

green, pink, red, and black construction paper

cotton balls

white glue

red yarn

scissors

red and white pipe cleaners

paper clip

Styrofoam tray to work on

hole punch

Here is what you do:

1. Cut two identical triangles from green paper with 4-inch (10-centimeter) bases and 6-inch (15-centimeter) sides. Cut two green rectangles for arms. Cut a head and hands from pink paper and boots from black paper.

2. Put glue all over one triangle. Put the tops of the boots in the glue at the bottom of the triangle. Glue the end of an arm about halfway down on each side of the triangle and glue a hand

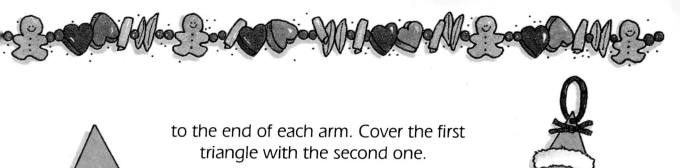

to the end of each arm. Cover the first triangle with the second one.

3. Glue the head about 2 inches (5 centimeters) down from the point of the triangle. Glue cotton across the top of the head, and glue a fluffed-out cotton ball on the face for a beard. Punch out eyes from black paper and cheeks and a nose from red paper and glue them in place.

4. Glue a piece of red yarn along the bottom of the triangle to trim the coat. Knot two short pieces of yarn and glue them to the front of the hat to form a tassel. Punch a hole in the top of the hat. String a long piece of yarn through the hole and tie the ends to make a hanger.

5. Twist two 4-inch (10-centimeter) pieces of pipe cleaner together to make a candy cane. Tie a yarn bow around the candy cane. Fold the elf's arms around in front to hold the candy cane and glue them in place. Use a paper clip to hold the arms together until the glue is dry.

Hand Reindeer

Santa uses flying reindeer to pull his sleigh full of toys.

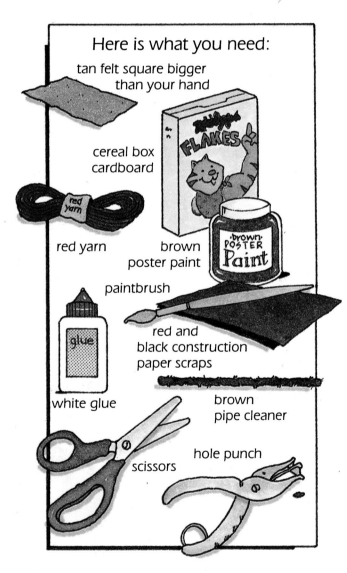

Here is what you need:

tan felt square bigger than your hand

cereal box cardboard

red yarn

brown poster paint

paintbrush

white glue

red and black construction paper scraps

brown pipe cleaner

scissors

hole punch

Here is what you do:

1. Glue the tan felt square to the print side of the cardboard cut from a cereal box. Place heavy weights, like books, on both sides of the cardboard so it dries flat.

2. Paint the palm side of your hand brown. Spread your thumb and fingers out and carefully print your hand on the felt. Let the hand print dry.

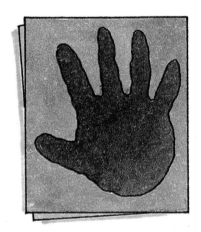

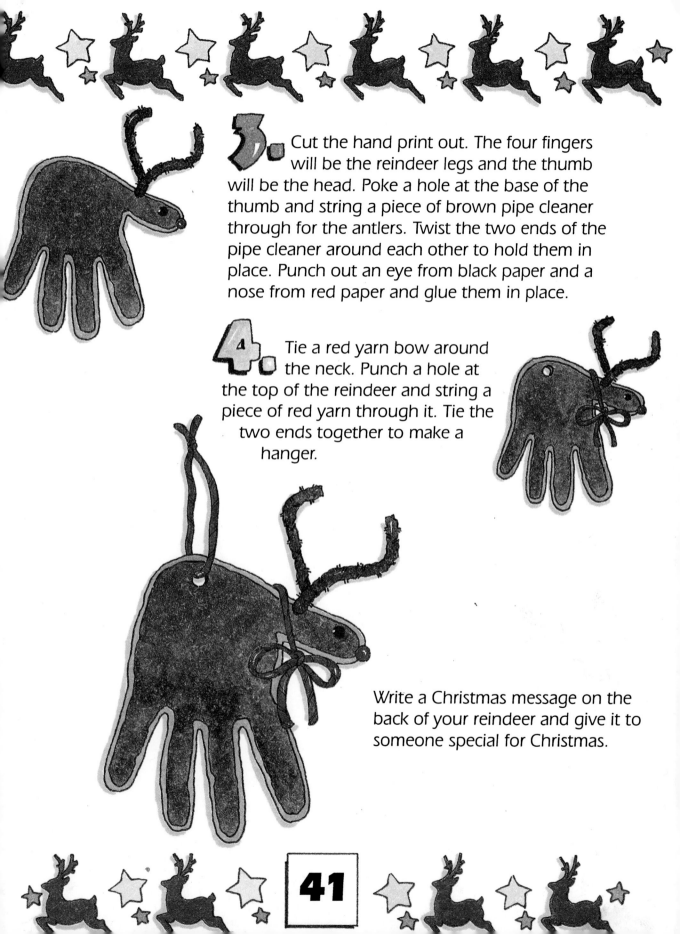

3. Cut the hand print out. The four fingers will be the reindeer legs and the thumb will be the head. Poke a hole at the base of the thumb and string a piece of brown pipe cleaner through for the antlers. Twist the two ends of the pipe cleaner around each other to hold them in place. Punch out an eye from black paper and a nose from red paper and glue them in place.

4. Tie a red yarn bow around the neck. Punch a hole at the top of the reindeer and string a piece of red yarn through it. Tie the two ends together to make a hanger.

Write a Christmas message on the back of your reindeer and give it to someone special for Christmas.

Reindeer Treat Bag

If it is foggy on Christmas Eve, Santa asks a red-nosed reindeer to use his shiny red nose to light the way.

Here is what you need:

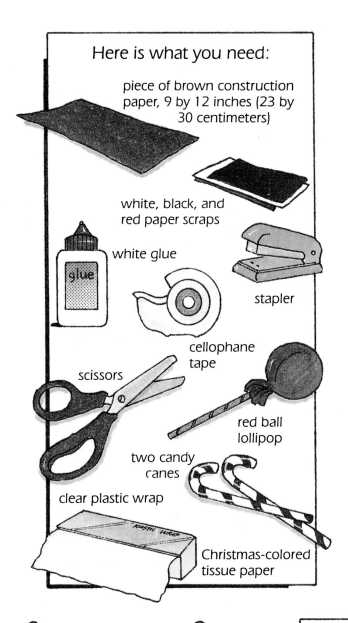

piece of brown construction paper, 9 by 12 inches (23 by 30 centimeters)

white, black, and red paper scraps

white glue

stapler

cellophane tape

scissors

red ball lollipop

two candy canes

clear plastic wrap

Christmas-colored tissue paper

Here is what you do:

1. Wrap the sheet of brown construction paper around itself lengthwise and form a cone. Staple the cone in place. Fold down the corners on each side at the top to form reindeer ears.

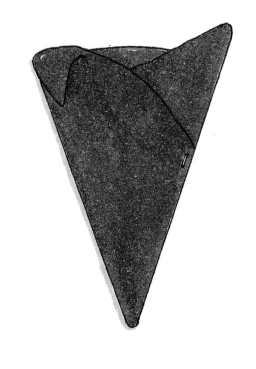

2. Cut eyes from white and black paper and glue them in place. Cut a handle from red paper and staple it across the top.

3. Unwrap the red lollipop and wrap it in clear plastic wrap to keep it clean. Slide the stick up into the hole at the point of the cone and tape the stick inside the cone so that the red ball forms the nose. Tape a candy cane inside the cone above each ear so that the hooks stick out to form the reindeer antlers.

Line the treat bag with Christmas-colored tissue and fill it with goodies to give to someone on your list.

Handprint Christmas Card

At Christmastime, many people send Christmas cards.
Here is a card that hangs on the tree.

Here is what you need:

cereal box cardboard

white poster paint

Christmas wrap with a small pattern

paintbrush

construction paper to match your wrapping paper

hole punch

red yarn

scissors

black marker

pinking shears

white glue

newspaper to work on

Here is what you do:

1. Cut out a piece of cardboard 5 by 7 inches (13 by 18 centimeters). Cover both sides with glue and then cover one side of the cardboard with construction paper and the other side with wrapping paper. Put something heavy on each end so that it will dry flat.

2. Paint the palm side of your hand with white paint. Spread your fingers and thumb slightly and carefully print your hand in the center of the wrapping paper. Let the print dry.

3. Trim around the cardboard with pinking shears to give it a nice edge. Punch two holes above the fingers of your hand and thread a piece of red yarn through the holes . Tie the two ends together to make a hanger. Glue a little bow of red yarn at the bottom of your hand.

Write a Christmas message on the back of the hand print and give it to someone who cares about you a lot.

Country Christmas Gift Bags

Gift bags are a pretty and easy way to wrap small gifts.

Here is what you need:

brown lunch bags

scissors

shaped cookie cutters

old sponge

two Styrofoam trays

red and green poster paint

red and green ribbon

light cardboard

newspaper to work on

hole punch

Here is what you do:

1. Make a stencil by tracing around a cookie cutter placed on light cardboard. Cut the shape out without cutting through the surrounding cardboard. Gingerbread boys, hearts, stars, and Christmas trees all work well for this project.

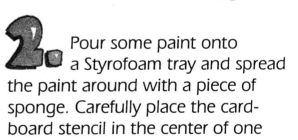

2. Pour some paint onto a Styrofoam tray and spread the paint around with a piece of sponge. Carefully place the cardboard stencil in the center of one

46

side of a flattened bag. Use the sponge to dab paint in the cut-out portion of the stencil. The shape of the stencil will appear on the bag. Make several different bags using different shapes and different colors of paint. Let the bags dry, then stencil the other sides.

Merry Christmas!

3. Fold the top of each bag over and punch two holes below the fold. String some pretty Christmas ribbon through the holes and tie it in a bow above the stenciled shape in order to close the bag.

Merry Christmas!
Love mike

If you wish, you can add details to your shapes using cut paper, sequins, or glitter.

About the Author and Illustrator

Twenty years as a teacher and director of nursery school programs have given Kathy Ross extensive experience in guiding young children through craft projects. Her crafts have appeared in *Highlights* magazine, and she has also written numerous songs for children. She lives in Oneida, New York.

Sharon Lane Holm won awards for her work in advertising design before shifting her concentration to children's books. Her illustrations have since added zest to books for both the trade and education markets. She lives in New Fairfield, Connecticut.

Kathy Ross and Sharon Lane Holm have collaborated on these additional craft books for kids: *Crafts for Kwanzaa, Crafts for Halloween, Crafts for Valentine's Day, Every Day Is Earth Day,* and *Crafts for Thanksgiving.*